BRIDGES TO FREEDOM & EQUALITY & KINDNESS

A Play by

PAULIE THE BALLIE

To order additional copies of this book, contact:
Bookwhip
1-855-339-3589
https://www.bookwhip.com

CONTENTS

_____

FOREWORD

This Play is loosely based on the first school integration shortly after Brown Versus The Broad of Education ruling in the November of 1960. Plus, A look at our framing of the Bill of Rights which set the stage for freedom and equality!

This is a work of fiction and I have changed names to preserve privacy. The play is focusing on the first year of that child's school life during those difficult times with a look at the protests and the kindness that under tremendous stress was offered to this 5-year-old Kindergarten black child. This story is an extraordinary tale of love and compassion during such a vileness by those anti integration forces, there are several heroes to write about and what they say is purely from this writer's imagination. This work is dedicated to all the pioneers of integration that stood bravely alone against demonic forces of hate and vileness. Not to forget that during this real life struggle some casualties came about and looking back we feel sad that this occurred but their sacrifice was not in vain. For only good things have resulted that have gone to benefit so many during the past 60 years. This a story of hope and dedication to the premise that all peoples have the right to pursue their lives equally under the law. I personally want to thank those gallant doers who enable this child to succeed and eventually become a pillar of that very place where it all transpired. Plus, a look at the genesis of that great Bill of Rights creator James Madison & his First Lady Dolley heroic tenure

Acknowledgments to John Steinbeck's Travels with Charley: Published by Viking Press 1962

CAST OF CHARACTERS

- The Bystander identified as a noted author
- Mary Lou the five-year-old youngster
- Mother of the child
- Lead Marshal in charge Mr. Goodman
- First day teacher Ms. Lovely
- Cheerleader 1 lead agitator
- Cheerleader 2
- Cheerleader 3
- Dr. Smiley child psychologist
- Parent of white child Mr. Adams
- Reporter local newspaper in New Orleans
- Noted Author and his hitchhiker
- Adult Mary Lou & Author with Bubba the Puppet
- President James Madison & His valet Paul Jennings
- Dolley Madison rescue of the Art Work of President George Washington
- Actor John Garfield & House Hearing Attorney anonymous

Props & Setting

Play opens up at Mary Lou's home in New Orleans.

Limo with four Marshals in front of their house

Franklin Grade School near the center of downtown New Orleans

Noted bystander in cab to the School. And later his R.V. with a hitchhiker

President James Madison & his Valet Paul Jennings

Dolley Madison in the White House hours before it was set ablaze by the British.

Actor John Garfield and Attorney for House Un American Hearing

ACT 1

Scene 1. Pick up for the ride to school

The noted author is riding in a cab to the school.

Cab driver says, "Wait to you sees those three ladies hold court and rile up the crowd. They sure are something to behold" Aside. "the noted author thinks surely they will take it easy on this 5-year kindergarten child." Then he replies to the Cabby, yes that why I came to see." Cabby replies, "you won't be disappointed".

The noted author had on a navy cap and thought he looked pretty unthreatening to the crowd and sure enough he was left alone pretty much. He positions himself not too far from the three cheerleaders who were screaming at the top of their voices, "Go back to home you are not wanted here bleep you and your family."

Then the crowd shouted here they come as the limo pulled in front of the school.

2 hours earlier, at the child's home.

Mother of Mary Lou is dressing her for the first day of school and says," Well my little angel that just about does it you look very nice. Today is your first day of a long journey which I know will be a success for you my child. Learning at a good school will only benefit you for making your way for a successful life. Any questions?" Mary Lou says, "Can I bring my teddy bear?" Mother replies, "Yes you may."

At that moment the Federal Marshals limo pulls up in front of the house. Four Marshals walk up to the door. The lead Agent is Mr. Goodman who has a determine look about him but also a look of compassion for his soon to be ward for the next few weeks. Introductions are done and the Lead Marshal says, "We will accompany the child to the front entrance through the crowd of protestors who will be across the street behind barriers we predict they will only be verbal protests but we will be on the alert for anything else. Okay let's go." Both the Mother and the child went with them this first day.

As the limo pulled in front of the school the crowd became very loud with some chants too obscene to mention here: Aside of the crowd, "Blah, blah, blah etc."

Mary Lou heard all the commotion and thought to herself (aside). "It must be a Mardi Gras celebration as she has seen crowds like this during those celebration." As they approach the entrance one could barely see the child who was surrounded by the four Marshalls. Her outfit was a stunning white dress neatly pressed with recently darned socks by Mama. Aside from Mary Lou, "One potato, two potato, three potato, with every stride then whoops a big skip to four potato." The Bystander aside, "She's playing a game and probably skips like that every so often when walking, and at that moment he knew this child will be okay as the confidence of innocence is very evident here. Amazing to see this happen with all the hate being eschewed by the crowd. She paid little heed to the noise and saw a smiling lady at the door with her arms outstretch to give her a very warm reception.

Lead Marshal aside, "He noticed with pride her demeanor and noticed there was no fear present a very brave trooper and he would cherish this moment for the rest of his life".

Cheerleader 1 aside," She thought to herself with each obscenity and the resulting roar from the crowd a kind of sexual excitement and said this is better than sex. She couldn't wait to get home and watch it all unfold on T.V. nightly news. For this moment put some meaning to a rather dull existence as she is a victim of domestic abuse and currently living alone".

Scene 2. The welcome

The teacher says, "Welcome Mary Lou it so nice to see you we will go inside and start working on our ABC's and do some drawing's with crayons". They would spend the entire day together as no else showed this first day. That would change on day two when one brave white family came to school with their child with the crowd's disapproval. This relationship will last for one year and years later they will meet once again to share their memories. A very pleasant reunion with plenty of respect for each other! Mary Lou now grown up with a successful career and a college degree. The teacher who was fired after that first year for no good reason had obtain an important role at a Junior College and now was retired.

Scene 3. The second day at school

2nd day of school One white parent showed with his youngster. The child's father a descendent of John Adams our 2nd President was determined not to let a bunch of red necks interfere with his child's education. That father's aside, "As he walked his son into the building to the taunts of bleep lover his jaw was taunt and he thought what a display of horse poop. No way are these haters going to stop the law of the land. For the rule of law must be respected to survive anarchy. History tells us that when the rule of law is ignored, death and destruction is the result. He calls it creeping fascism and which nearly destroyed democracy during the 2nd World War. I am determined to fight this evil with all my might so help me God." Aside: "The bystander saw this and thought to make a note for his chronicle that he was writing during his coast-to-coast trek of the Land for the American spirit".

Scene 4. One Month later session with counselor

One month later a counselor Dr. Smiley was called as Mary Lou was having some difficulty sleeping at night. He was a bright and positive man of science and immediately offer his service freely. He also helps with clothing as his children had out grown them. So, Mary Lou had one fine wardrobe. Aside from Dr. Smiley thought, "It is remarkable that Mary Lou is eager to attend school as the crowd is still showing up to protest one-month into the school term. But their numbers are less and eventually they will cease to show. He uses a simply approach with his counseling a very supported role and encouraging Mary Lou to voice any concern's which he adeptly deals with. His therapy does the trick and a full night sleep is now occurring." After his 1st week he brought a small little puppy after getting permission from the parents who was about 4 weeks old from a litter from his own dog a mixture of beagle and terrier. Mary Lou was thrilled and started to hug him and the puppy responded with several licks as it was instant bonding. Dr smiley asked, "what name are you going to give him"? and Mary Lou said without hesitation, "Happy", "That's a fine name for sure".

Scene 5. End of the first year

Full attendance at this age went well for the most part as these aged children were pretty void of racial bias. It would change later as the group aged but, on the whole, it was accomplished. Acceptances usually comes with experienced and is a hopeful sign that racial bias can indeed be modified. With that in hand we want to share the parting of the teacher and her students during the last day of school. Ms. Lovely says, "I like to congratulate everyone who attended school this year under some stressful times. History was in the making right here in New Orleans and I am proud to have been a part of that. I cherish the chance that was presented to me. I wish you a fond farewell as I have been told my services are no longer needed here at Franklin school. As each of you continue with your education, I hope I have encouraged you to have an inquiring mind to all the information that will be presented each year. I hope we have opened that portal for learning that will be so important to each of you to succeeding with your studies so I am giving you a letter to take home for your parents to read thanking them for your attendance here a Franklin school with a comment for each about your efforts. So, goodbye everyone I send my love, Ms. Lovely." In attendance were the parents and at that point a hearty round of applause was heard." Mary Lou had a tear in her eye.

ACT 2

Scene 1. Press release from Local reporter

The local reporter wrote this in his column summing up this first year of integration. Aside by the young reporter a descendant of Horace Greeley. "A landmark occurrence right here in New Orleans after so very stressful protests, the rule of law prevailed. A child of color was put through the wringer of hate and vileness that no human being should have to endure. Many came to her aid and a victory over these hateful acts was achieved. These gallant heroes have contributed to creating a path for many other children of color to attend good school gaining important knowledge that they will need in a very challenging world. History will be kind to these dedicated doers and those vile protestors will be quickly forgotten. So, let this victory resonate throughout this great land as we honor all who contributed to Mary Lou's attendance. One thing is for sure the quest for equality in learning has begun and God Bless this Great Country." This reporter will receive the Pulitzer prize and move up North to work for the New York Times.

Scene 2. Current times and some reflection on the matter at hand

So, the noted author saw this column and included his own experience in his book which became a best seller. His account focused on the means of dealing with racism and some hope that progress can be achieved with this complex dilemma that has been with the institution of slavery some 400 years ago. Aside by this noted author," Just maybe reparations will be strongly considered for this horrible denial of freedom for so many which is so overdue. It is only fitting that injustice be settled for all who ancestors paid for as slaves at no fault of their own. Torn from their roots and love ones in such a brutal manner must be acknowledged. It is the right thing to do so this Nation can move on as a moral and just Land. That is our prayer."

Aside from noted author, "As he drove away from this town, he voiced concern about what he had witnessed. Blatant racism that was so ugly that it, made him sick to his stomach. Going down the highway he saw a local with his thumb up as his faithful dog whimpered, he slowed down to offer him a ride. The young man was a rugged looking person who had several tattoos on his arms. He immediately offers this, "Did you see those nigger's try to get in that school?" The author replied yes, I did but he could not refrain from saying. It was a terrible time in our history not for the child's attendance as per the recent ruling by the courts but the vile reaction so many bigots displayed." The man replied," I see you are a niggar lover with a threatening look about him." The Author came to a sudden stop and told this man to get out of his vehicle." The man replied. "You going to make me." "The author took his arm and reach for something under the seat and the man replied okay, okay and gets out of the car screaming niggar lover, niggar lover." As the author drove away, he looked in the rear-view mirror and saw him shouting this over and over." "Time to head home he said".

Finale: The Reunion

So that first year comes to a close It is only fitting that the participants come together years later on that Monday in November. Meeting at that school once again. No catcalls now and it is a beautiful Fall day. Aside from a grown-up Mary Lou as she approaches the entrance once more, she says, "One potato, two potato, three potato, and skip to four potato and once again she sees a smiling face of Ms. Lovely. They have a big hug and Ms. Lovely says," So nice to see you." Several moments were shared once again. The ultimate triumph of that day has resonated through this Nation and Mary Lou (Aside) "Express her gratitude to all who came to that little 5-year-old assistance. For countless children would follow her steps that fateful day. Opening opportunities for some many other children of color! History will be very kind to those gallant enablers that stood so tall against the bigotry and hatred."

Then with arm and arm the full cast we see them singing, "One potato, two potato, three potato and skip to four potato. We are on the way to equality and justice and shall overcome.

Scene 3: The truth of matter and the lessons learned from this inspiring saga

As we wrestle with demigods and racial problems, we see a spark of hope with the young generation who are taking to the streets with a cry for social justice.

This movement needs our support so this author is asking those in the audience who agree with this quest to stand up and express their thoughts on the matter. One graying lady rises and says this, "In honor of my grandchild who died because of this hatred we need to stand up to this evil and I pray for all well-meaning peoples to join this crusade for never was there a more noble cause and we can overcome so help us God". "The audience rises up with a standing ovation chanting Yes, we can"!

In closing the following Act 2 is Act 3

An adult Mary Lou enters stage and says this," Thank you attending this our play. We hope you have enjoyed it". I like to introduce the Author and his pal Bubba.

ACT 3

_____

Scene 1. Pops & Bubba also make an appearance

Paulie The Ballie is sitting to the right in a chair and Bubba a puppet is on his knee. Spot light switches to them.

Pops says, "A writer's lament is not having his readers taking the time to glance at his endeavors! I write for them and only for them by spreading some safer ways to live under the ☀! It is a mission that is a reminder that life is precious and finding someone to love gives meaning to that living! Hoping to share what history has taught us to achieve a more peaceful world in the future for our children ☺ to grow up in is why I write! My humble efforts have been inspired by the following great writers: Erich Fromm, Arthur Miller, John Steinbeck, Herman Melville, Emile Zola, Charles Dickens whose Tiny Tim was the inspiration for Bubba! Truly it's been adventurous journey living in the literature of those great authors! It is my humble task to try to join that great crowd in some sort of achievement to echo their message of hope during these harrowing times! I pray for divine guidance to do so! Thank you for reading! It is a noble and rewarding. God Bless you everyone! Amen 🎧 to that Bubba".

Bubba says, "Here is why we choose the 6 authors above, Take Dr. Fromm first. His thoughtful essay's on Human Destructiveness is the truth of the matter showing what the root cause of mass shooting and blames it on very sick individuals who are unable to handle their depression and are in an extreme stage of Boredom. He offers ways to soften those tragic actions by having a strong sense of hope for society that is clearly on display".

2; Pops says, "Go on Bubba this sounds good".

"Okay Pops Arthur Miller works show this, his lead character in Death of a Salesman shows his grasping of false values and his inability to share and expressed love to his family lead him on a path to his demise"! Pops says, "Wow what a tragedy". Bubba answers, "Yes there is a little of Willy Lowman in everyone".

3. Pops says. "Now to my favorite Mentor John Steinbeck". Bubba says," Yeah mine too. Mr. Steinbeck was a genius of showing the human condition with all of its hardships and a cry for justice during hard financial times during the Great Depression. A classic tale of the striving of displacement of folks due to the dust bowl out West in the early thirties. When reading this story, you strangely became one of those folks and felt their sorrow and misery"!

4. Pops says, "Now the best narrator of literature Herman Melville" Bubba says, "Yup I agreed his poetry in his writing is classic and well construed. His Moby Dick explores how man question's God and his purpose and how when man challenges that and is hopefully unable to compete and fails miserably".

5. Pops says, "Number five is a very interesting as Emile Zola fought against tremendous odds and won the battle but lost the war as he was thought to have been poisoned causing his early demise. His overturning the verdict in that military trial was a hard-fought battle and showed that justice must be served and his article, I Accuse shows that writing can indeed played a role in obtaining justice".

6. Pops says, "Now the rare talent of Charles Dickens whose characters leap up off the pages and grasp the readers with recognition of a lot like their own traits. The redemption of Scrooge is literature finest moment and give us hope that yes things can change for the better".

7. Bubba concludes with this, "Literature has a definite role to play as each generation comes to grip with society's ills. It is a tool to show what path must be taken for practical solutions so that our children can live in peace and harmony.

Scene 2. Time frame during the War of 1812

President Madison was the first President to participate in war hostilities. This is an account of that historic event. His valet, Paul Jennings is summoned to the White House several days before and Paul says this, "Yes Sir I have brought the dueling pistols as requested with ample powder for loading". President Madison all of 5"4" and weighing some 100 pounds was all dressed in black says," Good man now let's get to the nearest garrison". They hasten to that prearranged location and the President says this, "Yes we are going to win this war so we can say to the British we will no longer tolerate your hijacking of our ships of commerce and will bring your acts of wars to task". The troops respond with "Hep, Hep, Hooray". One year later at the battle of New Orleans, General Jackson was triumphed setting up the treaty to be signed.

This is lesson of our history is important to relate as it was the start of our democracy as President Madison was so much a part of writing the articles of the United States Constitution that has lasted for over 260 years!

Scene 3. White House West Wing on August 24: 1814

Dolley Madison is with her staff getting ready to evacuate the White House as the British are on the March and due in a matter of hours. As they make the last-minute preparations what to take with them is the question? So, the favorite portrait of President George Washington was removed by Dolley's orders and neatly wrapped in canvas for the 4-hour trip to the safe house. Dolley says to the staff, "Please remain calm and we will get through this crisis". It was noted that her calming demeanor won the day and save that work of art from destruction! The head staff member said this, we all were assured by our lady's calmness and thank her deeply for that".

Furthermore, history will say that the time Dolley was First Lady set the tone for the future first Ladies who were inspired by her classic act of demeanor & performance. Dolley led the chorus for them in song during the trip (music of the times is heard in the background La, La, La and more)! After they arrived safely Dolley was heard to say." Your loyalty to this mission will not be forgotten and I am sure the President will acknowledge your support in an official condemnation". All received a personal letter of gratitude by President Madison and copies can be viewed in the Library of Congress!

Scene 4. Hearing room in Washington D.C.

Fast forward to the early 50's in Washington D.C. Place the House Hearings of Un American Activities

The Clerk speaks to the witness standing at the witness table he is John Garfield the Actor

The Clerk, "Please raise you right hand, do you swear to tell the truth and nothing but the truth"?

The Actor replies, "I do so swear".

The lead Lawyer for the panel asks, "Are you a member of the Communist Party"?

The Actor says, "I am not".

The lead lawyer continues," Please name anyone that you have knowledge of is a member of the Communist Party.

The Actor reply's" I will not answer that question and you have no right to request such a thing which you know it will destroy anyone and I will not be a part of that sir I am a proud American with liberal views and a loyal Democrat also I am not a Pink o or any similar color".

The Lead Lawyer says this, "Answer the question will you give us names of such affiliations and if you do not answer we censure you as a result".

The Actor and again refuses to answer. "No "!

In a few months after this he has not work in months in movies but does a stint on Broadway to rave reviews. Soon he will die of a stress ridden heart attack that his family blames on his harsh treatment by the House panel Un American activities! Truly a talented man of convictions who is wronging condemn for his beliefs. Another American tragedy with many more to come by these reactionary forces of the far right that is a very much a part of the current policy scene as we complete this war of ideas during this past Presidential election. So, Bubba the beat goes on and on. Just maybe we will learn from all this and move on to Freedom, Equality and Kindness as over 80 million kind souls dug down deep to support those very ideas this last election. God Bless this diverse land of immigrants!

With this in hand we have seen some positive proof that things have changed since that war of 1812! So, all the cast members join arms inter lock and singing we are now one nation of immigrants looking for cooperation to come together so this swirling planet survives as, "The United States of America"!

AFTER THOUGHT
FOR OUR PLAY

Pops aside, "Hey Bubba one more thing as we close this our Play. Let's tell the folks who you represent". Bubba reply's, "You have my permission". "Who is Bubba"? My main character in both of my Endeavors. Including, Under the Palm Tree.? An interesting question. Just who is our lead character Bubba? After some serious thought here, it is. Bubba represents the Common Man & Woman, the mail delivery person, the retail clerk, the factory worker, the law enforcement officers, first responders, nurses, teachers, Government workers who help keep us safe and protect our food and environment and air safety while travelling. All who are living from pay check to pay check. We see and deal with them daily and for the most part they are recognized as an important segment of our Society. Bubba strives to see the good that is inherent in all well-meaning peoples. He is very much on his own and how he succeeds depends a lot on who represents us. He is ever Hopeful and tries his best to make the correct choices during his life's journey., There are however some destructive forces at work that need tending to and Bubba sees this and wants to do something about it. Too many are in harm's way. He wants to change some miss conceptions and better protect the public at large. His message is loud and clear to sound the alarm for a safer place for our children to grow up in, having hope for a better future is so important to maintain and must not be put asunder. That is his message. Pops says, "Do you think Bubba, I got it right"? "Yup right on the money you old fart". "It is only fitting that this Play shows the heroic history of our young Republic as so many showed a firm commitment to freedom and equality for all walks of life. Our work here hopefully tells part of that gallant saga". Bubba & Pops says, "So Long Folks and have a great journey everyone and keep the faith"

January 6th 2021 A poem for that Fateful Day: Pops read's this as the last word for this our play.

O Captain, O Captain, what have you done?

Blown a hole in our ramparts of democracy I hear many say releasing demons of venom and hate. My God will we restore our freedoms and fate? Yes, we will as years gone by, we always get back to our values and will abide to say we are once again standing strong as the United States of America and together we will strive for freedom and justice for all for that's our way I hear the majority say and those doubters will come back to the fray so help US God this day! P/S This poem is dedicated to Brian Sicknick and all who died that fateful day January 6th another day of infamy!'

EPILOGUE

A tale of courage that needs to be told this age of social unrest. This tale is based on military action during the Great War in the year of our Lord 1918. It is a gallant display of courage under tremendous odds by two black soldiers but is really about Sgt Henry Johnson medal winning acts that strangly never received the credit that it deserved. It took 10 decades for that Congressional Medal of Honor to be awarded. It is a honor to tell his story once again. So let it rip Bubba!

He and his buddy on guard duty that dark night helping the French Garrison flank! They were standing alert when they heard a faint noise from that hill to left and the steel point helmet of the enemy reflected from the moon as it broke through a cloud! As this exploratory squad of twelve came before the main company of many assaulted them! They responded killing the four lead insurgents! And then it was hand to hand combat even with both had wounds but Henry was strong having done manual labor since a young age to subdued four more of the enemy in quick succession! He noticed his partner was hurt real bad and was in jeopardy to be taken prisoner so he made quick work at hand and grabbed his buddy with one arm a shooting his weapon with the other clearing a way to the rest of his unit saving the day as they sounded the alarm preventing serious lost of life to fight another day! His commander later would recommend the highest medal for extraordinary bravery under fire one can get! A piece of history that one needs to have as we fight for our freedoms as I write! Amen 🙏 to that Bubba

Sgt Johnson eventually received the following medals: The French Croix de guerre with a golden palm, Congressional Medal of Honor 100 years later as well The Distinguished Service Cross!

He died destitute in 1929!

What a gallant hero that young man was he deserves world wide recognition as I write. Amen to that Bubba!

I hope this shows the need to continue the previous heroic stands taken by so many in the struggle for

freedom, equality that have been told ihere in this
our play. It is only fitting to add this in closing,

To illustrate the truth of the matter that still is being
contested! We offer this! The first real examination
of the evil of slavery and what to do about it was the
extraordinary life of Harriet Tubman. Ms. Tubman
mobilized many rescue's of hundreds of slaves by
risking her own life leading those escapes to freedom!
This was extremely dangerous as those slave owners
were intent to capture her at all costs! Her exploits
finally were given the credit it so deserved last year
by a great film with fantastic directing and acting!
Then shortly thereafter the South succession and
the Civil War was on! A story of that 4 year battle
was told by Stephen Crane in his epic "Red Badge
of Courage"! The author showed in vivid detail the
senseless in putting so many lives in a death spiral
seldom experienced in this Nation's history! How
one fighter for the Union, Henry, felt about this
is brilliantly portrayed! He was able to overcome
panic and fear and by grabbing the symbol of why
we are fighting that being Old Glory the Stars and
Stripes he was embody to lead his fellow soldiers
to victory! So even if he was wounded his wound
would be a badge of honor for he was fighting for
a just cause freedom and justice for thousands of
falsely enslaved peoples! Ironically this battle still

rages on as I write! JANUARY 6th was a continuing of those same causes of 1865 conflict! Flags of the confederacy were again in display! I wonder what Mr. Crane would think about that 150 year's later! This war is foolishly killing more as I write! Have we at last not realized that war is an abomination of false ideology that some use to gain control and be elected to govern?

We as a Nation must castaway such demigods and do a better job of protecting our democracy or we shall be in jeopardy of losing all we hold dear! Amen 🙏 to that Bubba P/S Dedication to all who died that day of infamy January 6th

This final thought as Pop's take center stage his aside,"Today is definitely a time to share the thoughts of the greatest innovator of this century "Noam Chomsky "! We have been blessed to have this man amongst us! In spite of the support for Trump he still has hope to achieve the following relief for the American working class: 1. Action to stop the number one danger to this planet, global warming. 2. Universal health care. 3. Income equality by starting with an increase for the minimum wage to $15! Bubba and I agree 100% ! Our history tell us yes we will stand fast against the forces of fascism that now are festering in the Republican Party! He has one suggestion to win back those blue collar workers show them you care about their struggles and deliver on all of the above! Let the word go forth that the torch of freedom & progress has been once again passed to a new generation borne through a terrible miss handled pandemic killing thousands way before their time ! We highly resolve here to forge ahead and implement a safer environment for our children to grow up in ! So let that be the motto of the new Democratic Party and get the hell going so help us God! So all we have to do is cross that bridge that so many have built for us during our heroic past to have that new birth of freedom and equality and for sure kindness will follow! Amen 🐵 to that Bubba"

AUTHOR BIO

Paulie the Ballie lives on the West coast of Florida since 1994. He is married for 58 years he has two daughters and 3 Grands. Playing golf, the greatest game known to man and woman. He started to play this game at 10 years of age has given him so much. As it keeps one completive and young of heart. It is one of best ways to enjoy other people's company. This feeling of connection to others during these twilight years is so important. The Spirit of competing on the course is the best therapy as one can put aside any of his concerns that may be troublesome as the player's is only thinking of stroking that little dimpled ball into yon hole". He has written three endeavors which one has been republished with some minor additions that is Under the Palm Tree Take 2 soon to be release by Book Whip.com. And in the Light of Day published by Lulu.com. And now this Play," Y" published with BookWhip.com, a look at why we are here and just might be our destiny. A Second Play titled," Bridges to Freedom & Equality & Kindness", soon to be available with Amazon.

Plus, some comments on Main Street. U.S.A. with some glances back in time.

"Say so long Bubba". "So long folks and have a great journey"!

www.ingramcontent.com/pod-product-compliance
Lightning Source LLC
Chambersburg PA
CBHW022107020426
42335CB00012B/863